SCHIRMER'S LIBRARY
OF MUSICAL CLASSICS

Johann Sebastian Bach

The Well-Tempered Clavier

Forty-Eight Preludes and Fugues

For the Piano

Edited by

CARL CZERNY

With a Biographical Sketch of the Author by

PHILIP HALE

IN TWO BOOKS

→ Book I — Library Vol. 13
Book II — Library Vol. 14

G. SCHIRMER, Inc.

DISTRIBUTED BY

HAL•LEONARD
CORPORATION

7777 W. BLUEMOUND RD. P.O. BOX 13819 MILWAUKEE, WI 53213

JOHANN SEBASTIAN BACH, the greatest member of a large family of distinguished musicians, was born at Eisenach, March 21, 1685. His father, Johann Ambrosius Bach (1645-1695) was a violinist and an organist, and he married for his first wife, Elizabeth Lämmerhirt of Erfurt, who died when Sebastian, her eighth and last child, was about nine years old. After the death of his father, Sebastian was brought up and taught by his brother, Johann Christoph, organist at Ohrdruff; the boy had received violin lessons from his father, and, in all probability, clavichord lessons from his uncle, Johann Christoph. Stories are still

told of the jealousy of Sebastian's brother and the secret studies of the boy, who sang in the choir, and in 1700 received free education in Lüneburg, from which place he made excursions on foot to Hamburg, to hear the organists Reinken and Lübeck. About this time Bach became acquainted with the works of the French clavecinists ; and the influence of Couperin, the Great, is seen in many of his compositions for clavichord. We know little comparatively of the education of Bach ; but it is more than probable that he was essentially an autodidact.

Bach's first position was in 1703 as violinist in the orchestra of Prince Johann Ernst at Weimar. A few months afterward he was appointed organist of the New church at Arnstadt, in which town he staid four years. He visited Lubeck, and associated with Buxtehude, who influenced mightily his compositions for organ. In 1707 Bach moved to Müllhausen, where he played the organ and taught for a year. Here he was married to his cousin, Maria Barbara, by whom he had seven children, of whom four grew up. 1708 saw the couple in Weimar, where Bach was court organist and chamber-musician to the reigning duke, William Ernst, who was fond of church-music. Nine years were spent busily and agreeably in Weimar. In 1717 Bach entered the service of Leopold, prince of Anhalt-Köthen, and lived at Köthen where he had neither an organ to play nor a chorus to lead ; he devoted himself to orchestral and chamber music. His wife died in 1720 ; the next year he married Anna Magdalena Wülken, the daughter of a court trumpeter ; she sang, copied music, and bore her husband thirteen children, six of whom grew up ; she died in 1760, after living for eight years on public charity. Bach went to Leipzig in 1723 to fill the positions of Cantor at the Thomas School and musical director of the city. Here he labored for twenty-seven years. His eyes troubled him seriously during the latter years of his life, and at the end he was totally blind. He died July 28, 1750.

These are the baldest outlines of a life distinguished by enormous labor. We have no time to look at the contests with foreign virtuosos, the interest in new instruments, the parochial quarrels with petty officials, the intercourse with rulers. The man's life was one of counterpoint and household joy and care. His nature was sanguine ; his temper was stormy. He was aware of his own worth ; yet he was free from the common jealousy and vanity of musicians. A severe teacher, he was beloved by his pupils. He was robust, broad-shouldered, with highly developed forehead, deep eyes, good and large mouth : a face of keenness, frankness, and strength. The man was economical, honorable, yes, noble.

As a musician he summed up the past, exhausted his own age, and looked beyond even the end of this century. But we have not to do with the Maker of the Matthew Passion, the Mass and the church cantatas ; nor may we now regard the master of organ prelude and fugue ; we are concerned with the composer of "The Well-tempered Clavichord," sometimes called "the 48 preludes and fugues."

This work is in two parts, and each part contains 24 preludes and 24 fugues. The first part was finished in 1722 at Köthen, and to this part alone he gave the name "The Well-tempered Clavichord." The second part was finished in Leipzig, probably in 1744. It is believed that early compositions were used in the compilation of the first part, and it is certain that many preludes had already appeared as independent compositions.

Bach is said to be the introducer of our present system, the "equal temperament," but it was known probably before, as Mersenne gave the correct number of the ratios in 1636. In the first system of temperament, the "unequal" or "mean-tone," the more common scales were fairly accurate, the others were ignored. Our present system is a compromise, and the only interval tuned with accuracy is the octave. "The sharp of a tone and the flat of the tone that follows are regarded as identical." Bach here showed the possibilities of the new system.

A new system of fingering was introduced inevitably by this work. Before Bach, the little finger and the thumb were almost never used, for although Couperin gave in 1717 directions for using them, his manner is strange, at times inexplicable. J. A. Hiller tells us in his life of Bach (1784) that Bach employed all the fingers equally ; he had invented his own system of fingering for conquering difficulties, and it rested chiefly on the use of the thumb.

From the purely musical standpoint, these preludes and fugues are a monument for all time. As William Cart well says, this chaste Muse shuns the "screaming" light of the concert hall, nor will she speak to the jaded ears of a crowd indifferent, or greedy for startling effects. "Each of these pieces has its own cachet ; and you remember it, as the face of a loved one." Are some severe ? Others are full of modern romanticism. If Bach now pours out his soul in prayer, or gives way to gloomy thought, at other times he laughs with peasant gayety and dances and sings with the people. And often the most surprising contrapuntal feat escapes notice by the apparent simplicity of the performance. PHILIP HALE.

Preface.

The principal object in issuing this new edition of J. S. Bach's "Well-tempered Clavichord" has been to make it as correct and complete as possible, both by means of comparison with all preceding editions, and by collating with some earlier manuscripts. In marking the fingering, which renders this issue far more generally useful, two points have been steadily kept in view:

First, to keep the hands as quiet as may be, even in extremely complicated passages; Secondly, to enable the player to bring out each separate part independently, with perfect smoothness, and with due regard to the phrasing.

Patient study, either on the pianoforte or on the organ, will be rewarded by the rich and full effect produced by a smooth and flowing polyphonic rendering.

It has been my endeavor to indicate tempo and interpretation:

First, according to the unmistakable character of each movement; Secondly, according to the well-remembered impression made on me by Beethoven's rendering of a great number of these fugues; Thirdly, according to convictions matured by more than thirty years' study of this work.

Wherever an extremely rapid tempo is indicated, this is, of course, meant only for the pianoforte. When playing passages so marked on the organ, the tempo must be moderated very decidedly.

Those who have no Maelzel's Metronome at hand are reminded, that the Allegro in these old compositions is to be taken, as a rule, much more tranquilly and slowly than in modern works.

Vorwort.

Bei dieser neuen Ausgabe von J. S. Bach's wohltemperirtem Clavier hat man vor Allem gestrebt, durch Vergleichung aller frühern Ausgaben so wie einiger ältern Handschriften, die möglichste Correctheit und Vollständigkeit zu erlangen. In der Angabe des Fingersatzes, wodurch dieses Werk eine weit grössere Gemeinnützlichkeit erhält, wurde stets der zweifache Gesichtspunkt beachtet:

Erstens, die Hände, auch in den verwickeltesten Fällen möglichst ruhig zu halten; Zweitens, jede einzelne Stimme von den Andern unabhängig, streng gebunden und folgerecht ausführen zu können.

Der Spieler wird die daran zu verwendende Mühe, sowohl auf dem Pianoforte wie auf der Orgel, durch die gehaltreiche Wirkung belohnt finden, die mit einem vollstimmigen und fliessenden Spiele hervorgebracht wird.

Das Zeitmass und den Vortrag habe ich:

Erstens, nach dem unzweifelhaften Character eines jeden Satzes; Zweitens, nach der wohlbewahrten Erinnerung wie ich eine grosse Anzahl dieser Fugen einst von Beethoven vortragen hörte;

Drittens, endlich nach den Ideen aufzuzeichnen und zu bewahren gesucht, welche ich selbst durch ein mehr als dreissigjähriges Studium dieses Werkes in mir festsetzte.

Wo ein bedeutend schnelles Zeitmass vorgeschrieben wurde, ist es natürlicher Weise nur für das Pianoforte berechnet. Wollte man jedoch die so bezeichneten Sätze auch auf der Orgel vortragen, dann müsste allerdings das Tempo bedeutend langsamer genommen werden.

Für diejenigen, denen kein Maelzel'scher Metronom zu Gebote steht, wird noch erinnert, dass das Allegro bei diesen ältern Compositionen in der Regel viel ruhiger und langsamer zu nehmen ist, als bei modernen Tonstücken.

CARL CZERNY.

Inverted mordent.   Mordent.   Trill without after-beat.   Trill with after-beat.

Praller.   *Mordent.*   *Triller ohne Nachschlag.*   *Triller mit Nachschlag.*

Contents
Vol. I

Part First.

Preludio I.

Allegro. (♩ = 112.)

J. S. BACH.

All figures in the fingering which are set a-bove the notes are intended, whether in inner or outer parts, for the right hand; whereas, the figures below the notes are for the left hand. This explanation will suffice to show, in doubt-ful cases, by which hand any note in the inner parts is to be played.

Alle Fingersatz-Zahlen, welche über den Noten stehen, gelten (auch in den Mittelstimmen) stets der rechten Hand. Dagegen sind die unter den Noten stehenden Zahlen immer für die linke Hand bestimmt. Dieses reicht hin, um in zweifelhaften Fällen an-zuzeigen, von welcher Hand jede Note in den Mit-telstimmen gegriffen werden muss.

11015

Fuga I.
a 4 Voci.

Moderato e maestoso. ($\bullet$ = 116.)

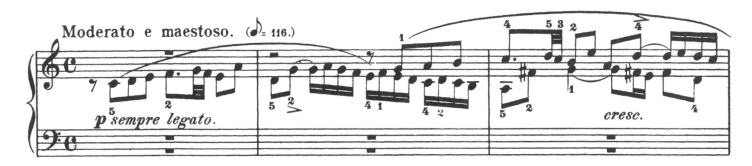

p sempre legato.   cresc.

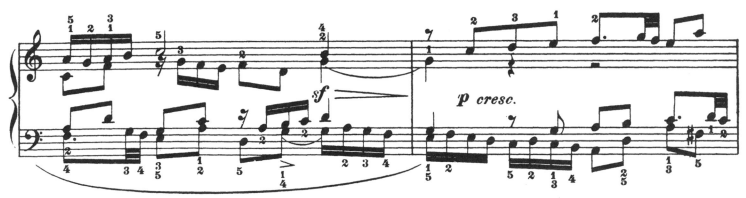

p cresc.

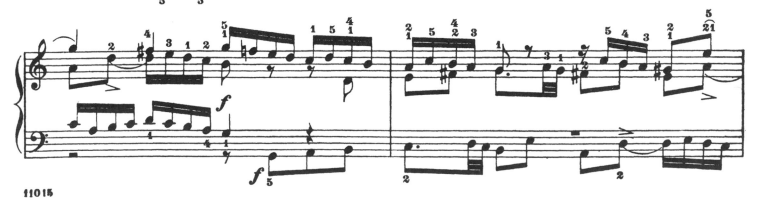

Preludio II.

Allegro vivace. (= 144.)

Fuga II.
a 3 Voci.

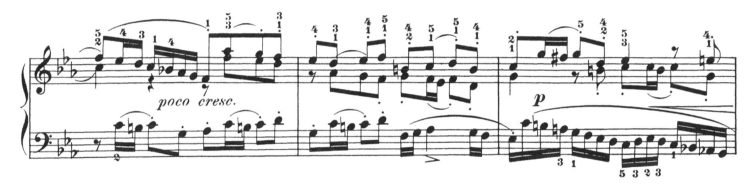

Preludio III.

13

11015

Fuga III.
a 3 Voci.

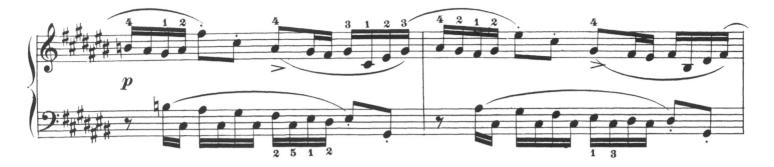

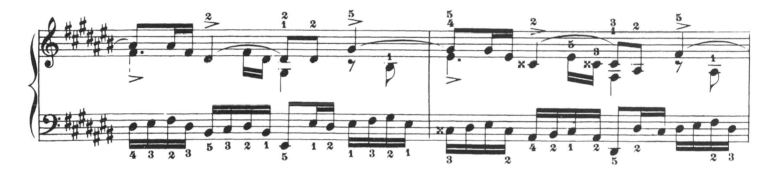

11015

Preludio IV.

Andante con moto. ($\quad$ = 92)

Fuga IV.
a 5 Voci.

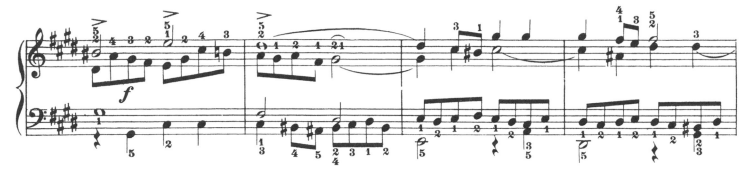

Preludio V.

Allegro vivace. (♩ = 132)

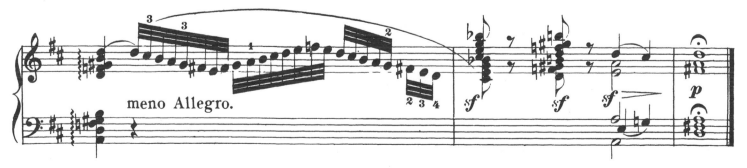

Fuga V.
a 4 Voci.

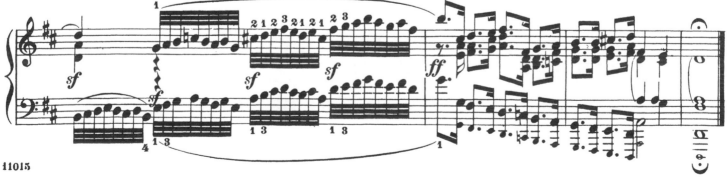

Preludio VI.

Fuga VI.
a 3 Voci.

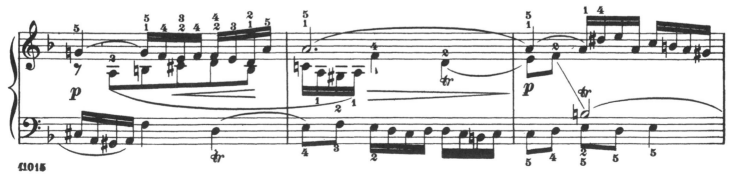

Preludio VII.

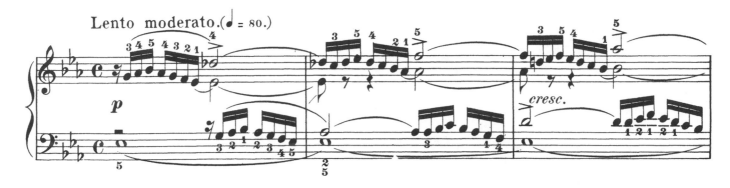

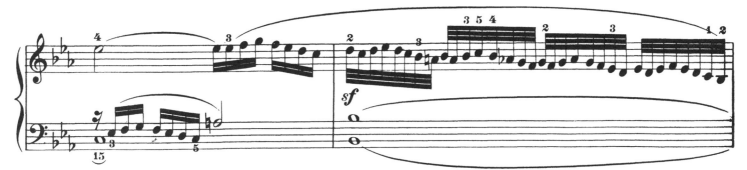

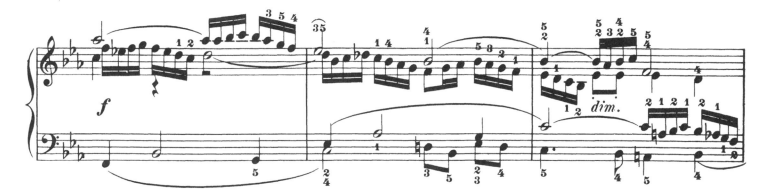

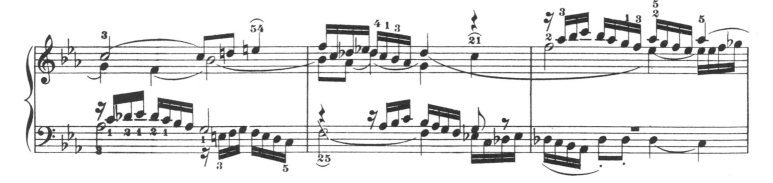

Fuga VII.
a 3 Voci.

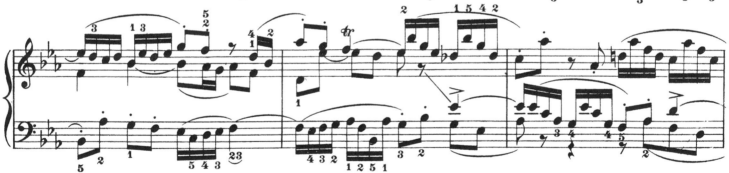

Preludio VIII.

11015

Fuga VIII.
a 3 Voci.

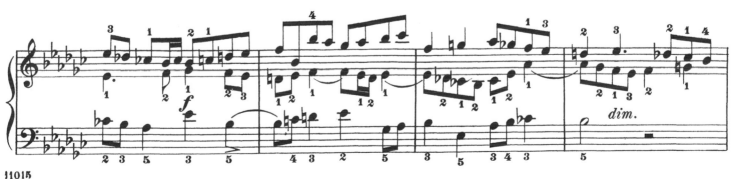

11015

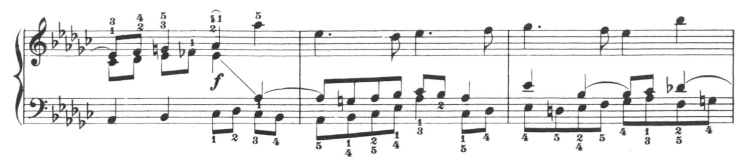

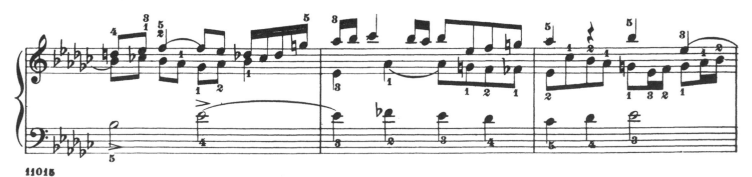

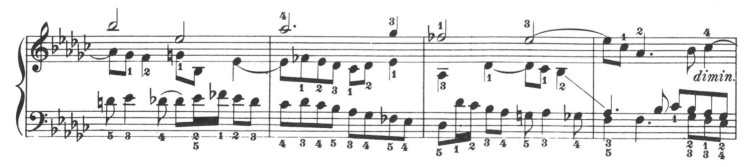

11015

Preludio IX.

Fuga IX.
a 3 Voci.

Allegro vivace. ($\bullet$=108.)

Preludio X.

Allegro molto moderato. (♩=84.)

Presto. (♩ = 80.)

Fuga X.
a 2 Voci.

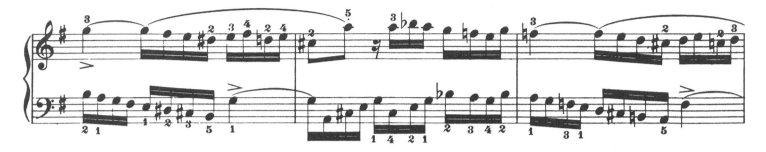

Preludio XI.

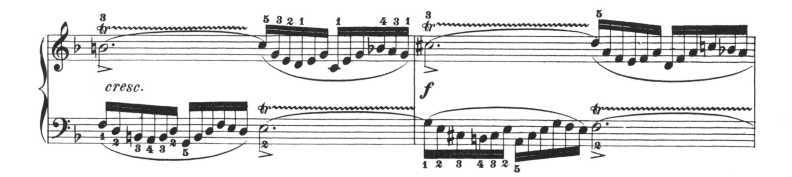

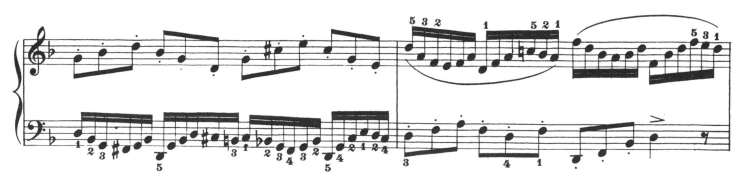

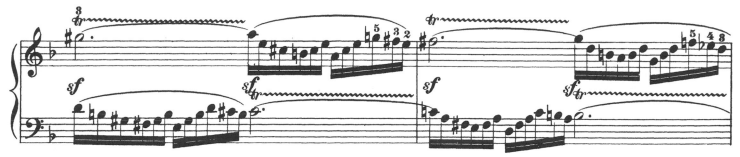

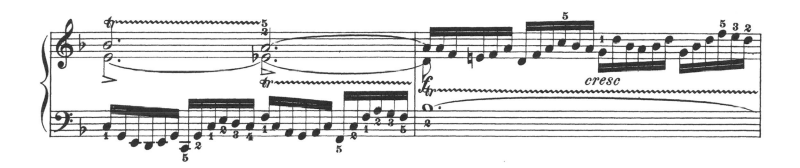

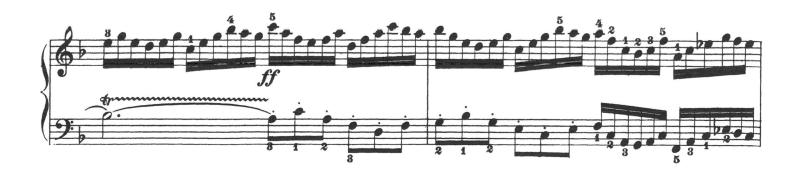

Fuga XI.
a 3 Voci.

Allegretto. ($\downarrow$.=66.)

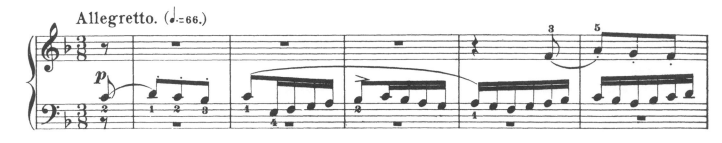

Preludio XII.

Andante espressivo. ($\flat$ = 104.)

Fuga XII.

a 4 Voci.

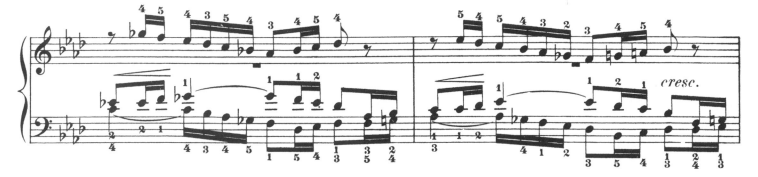

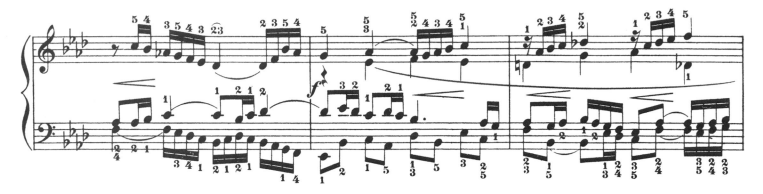

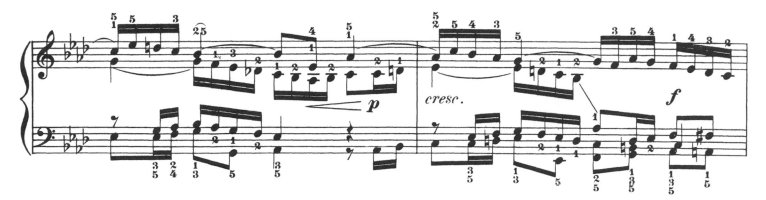

Preludio XIII.

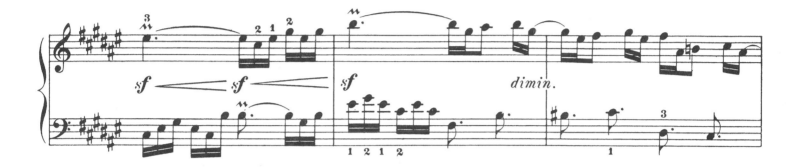

11015

Fuga XIII.

a 3 Voci.

Allegretto piacevole. (♩ = 88.)

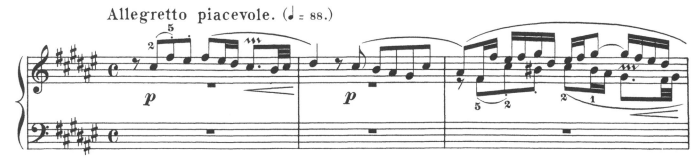

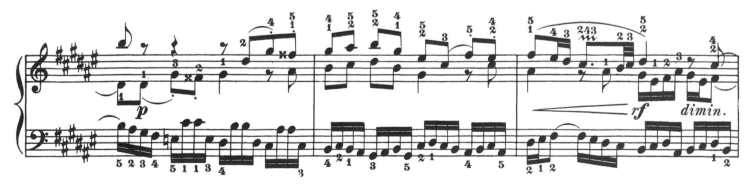

Preludio XIV.

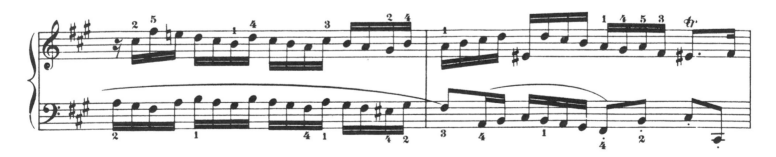

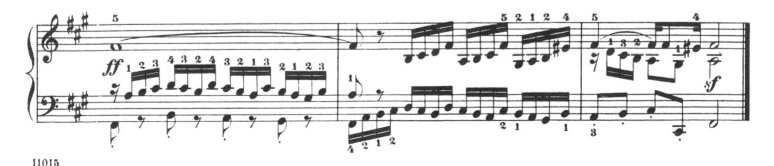

Fuga XIV.
a 4 Voci.

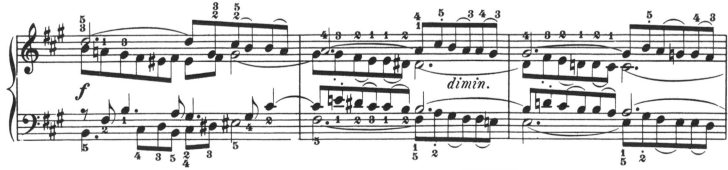

Preludio XV.

Allegro. (♩ = 100.)

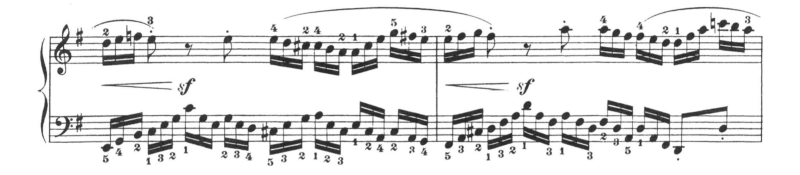

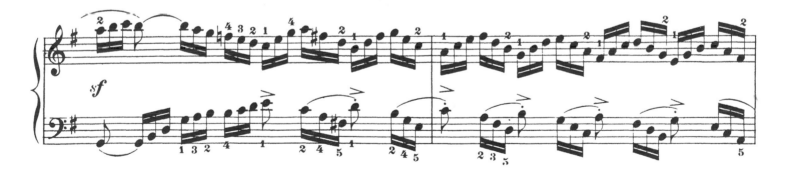

Fuga XV.

a 3 Voci.

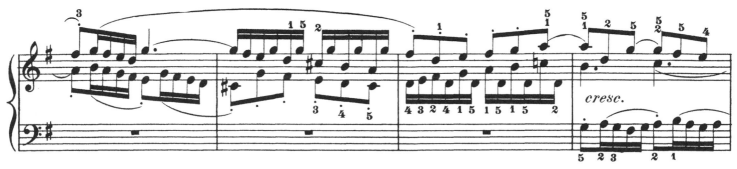

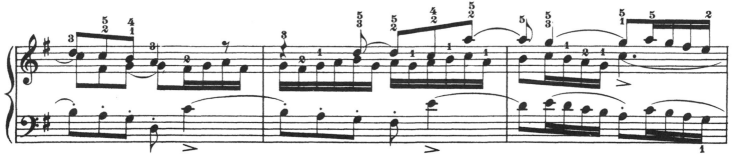

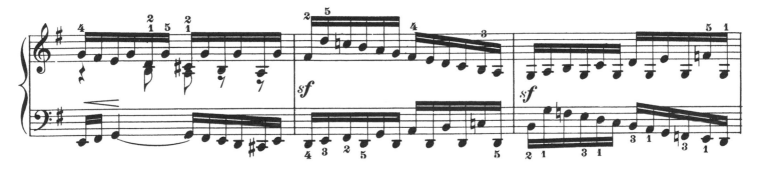

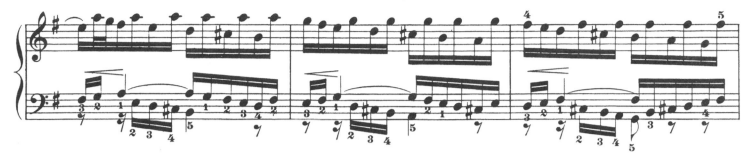

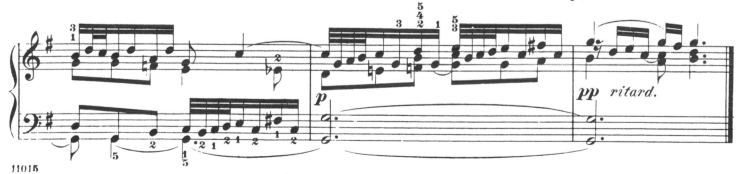

Preludio XVI.

Lento moderato. (♩=69.)

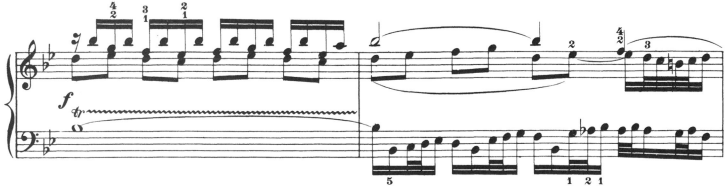

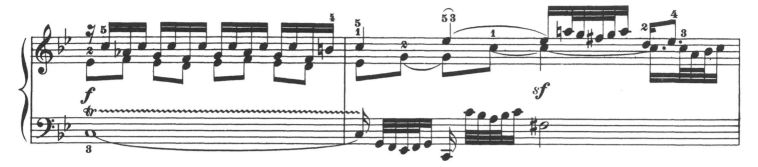

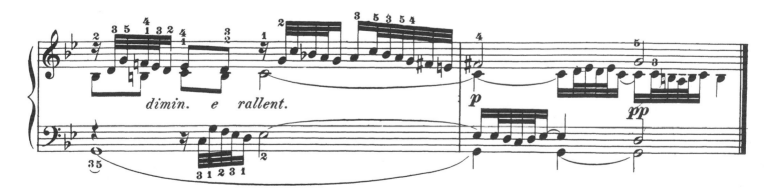

Fuga XVI.
a 4 Voci.

Andante con moto. ($\quad$=80.)

Preludio XVII.

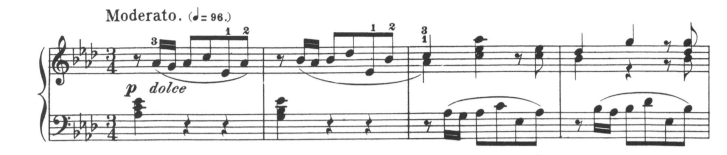

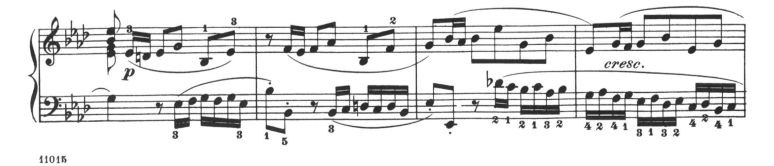

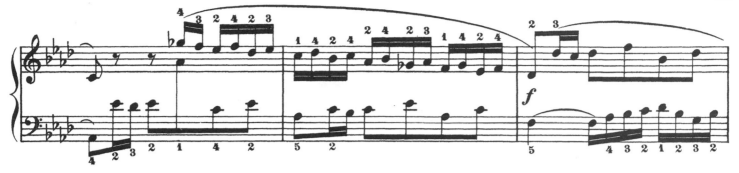

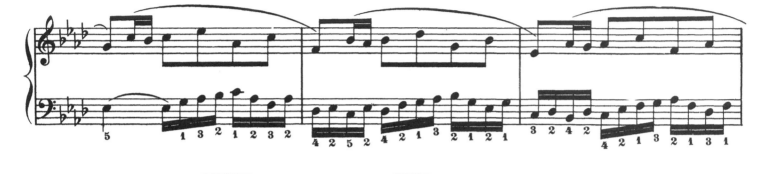

Fuga XVII.
a 4 Voci.

Preludio XVIII.

Allegretto moderato ed espressivo.($\flat$ = 126.)

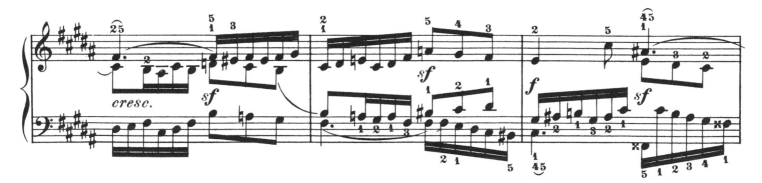

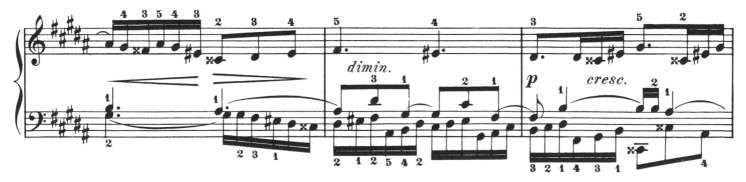

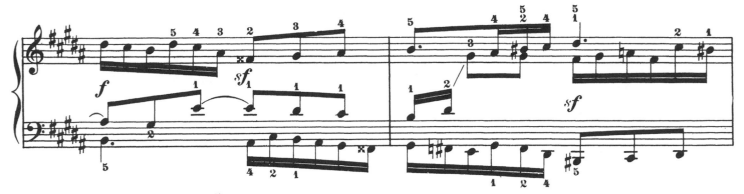

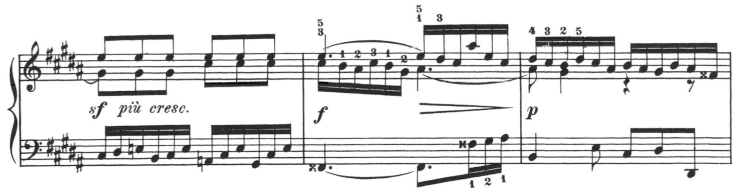

Fuga XVIII.
a 4 Voci.

Andante espressivo.($\flat$ = 108.)

Preludio XIX.

Fuga XIX.
a 3 Voci.

Allegro moderato. (♩.= 69.)

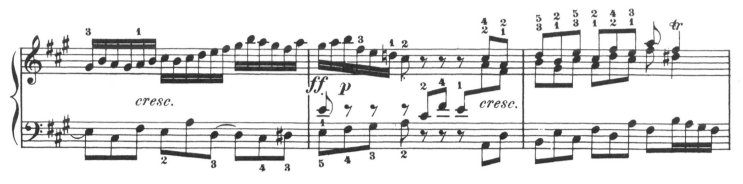

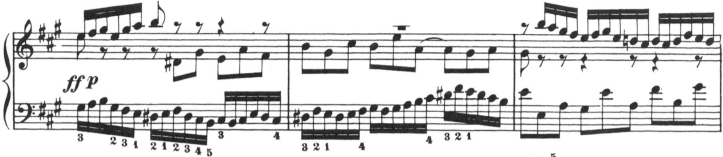

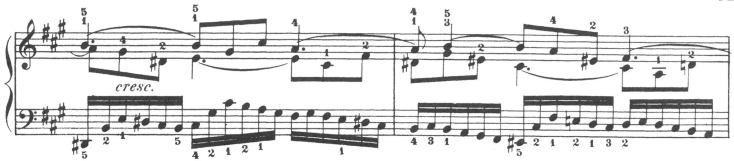

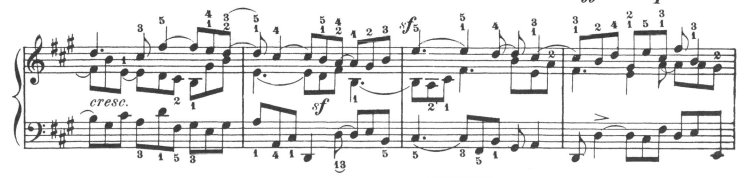

Preludio XX.

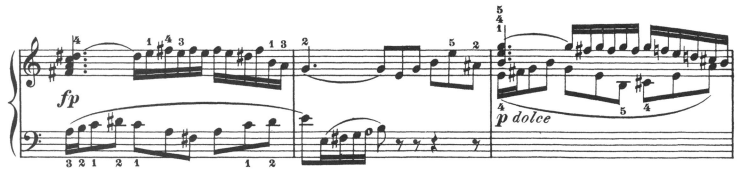

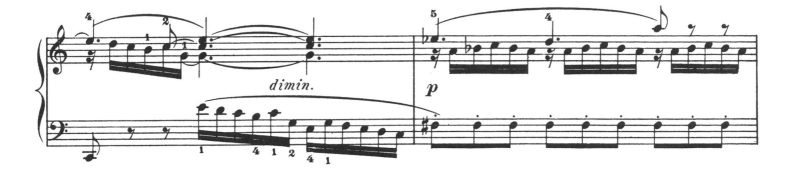

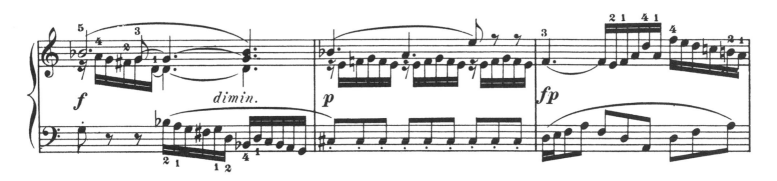

Fuga XX.

a 4 Voci.

Andante maestoso, ma con moto. ($\quad$ = 72.)

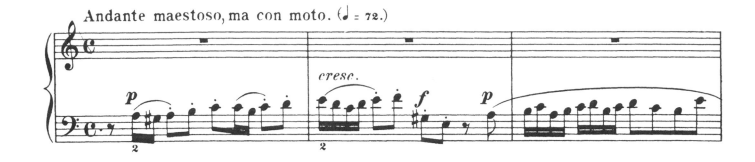

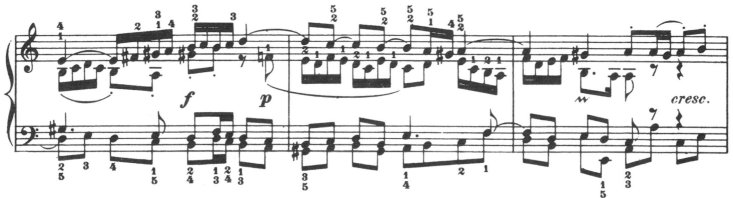

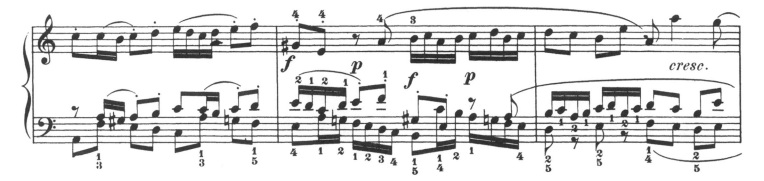

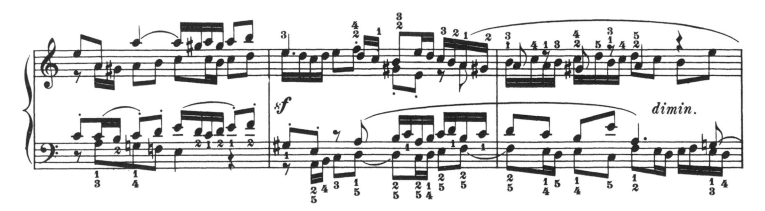

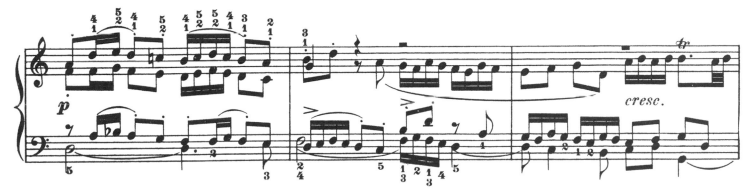

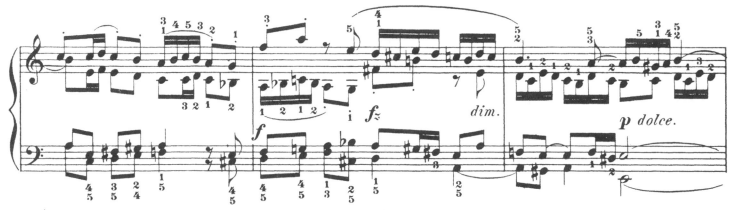

Preludio XXI.

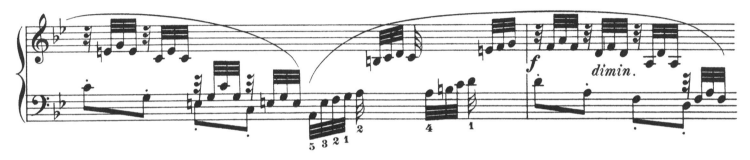

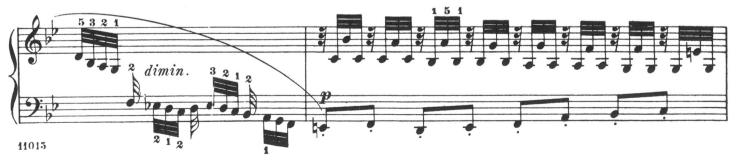

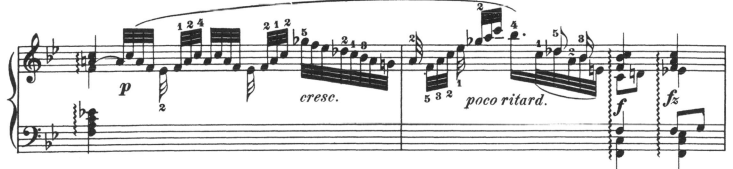

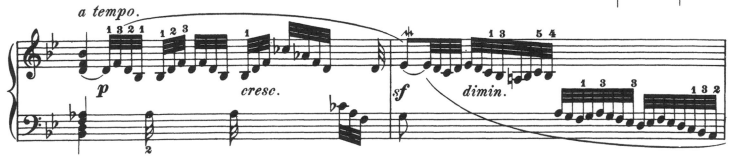

Fuga XXI.
a 3 Voci.

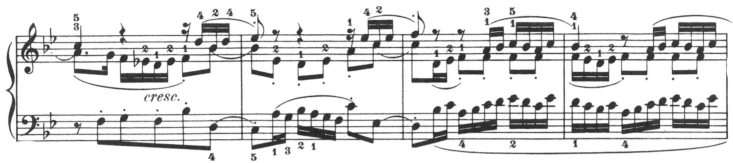

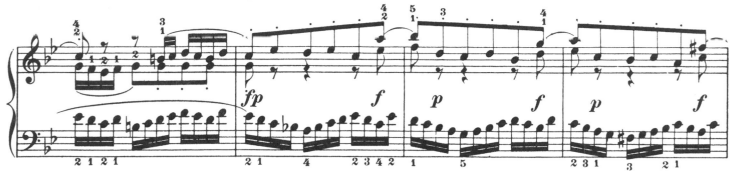

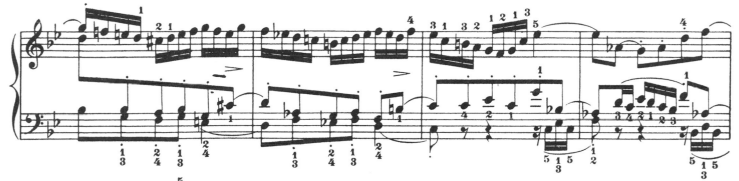

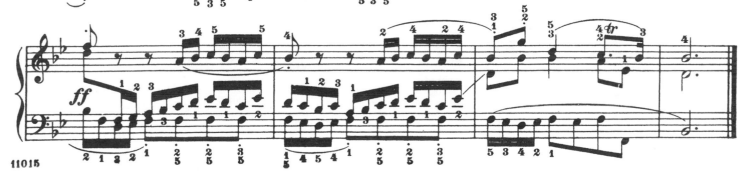

11015

Preludio XXII.

Andante sostenuto. ($\quad$ = 92.)

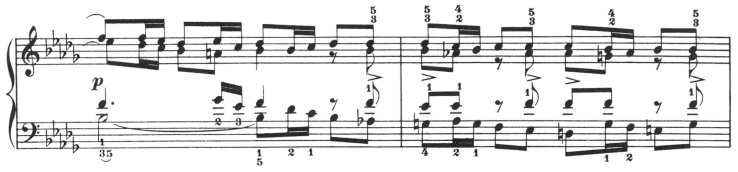

Fuga XXII.
a 5 Voci.

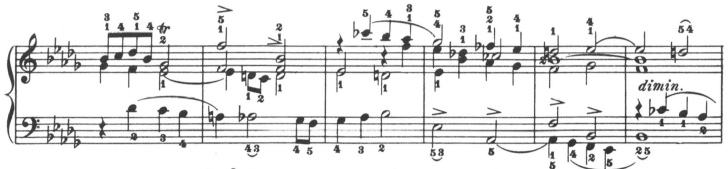

Preludio XXIII.

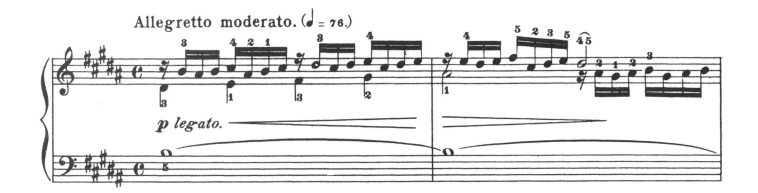

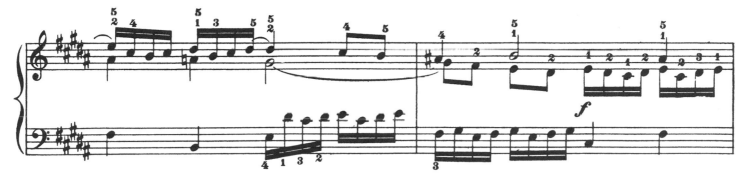

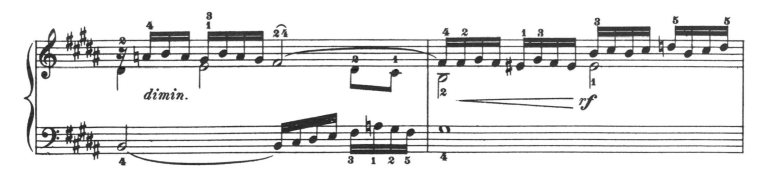

Fuga XXIII.
a 4 Voci.

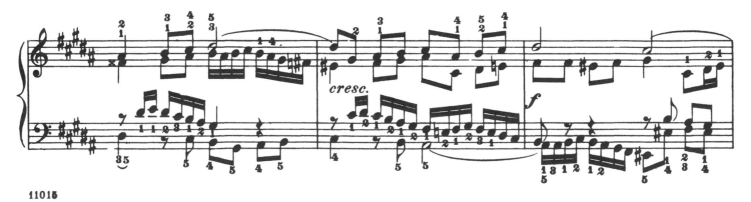

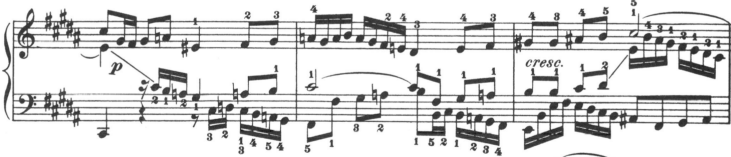

Preludio XXIV.

11015

Fuga XXIV.

a 4 Voci.

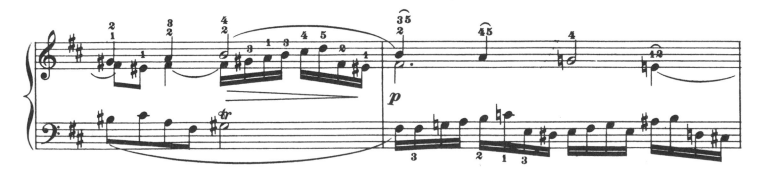

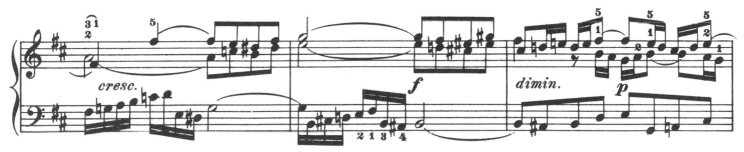

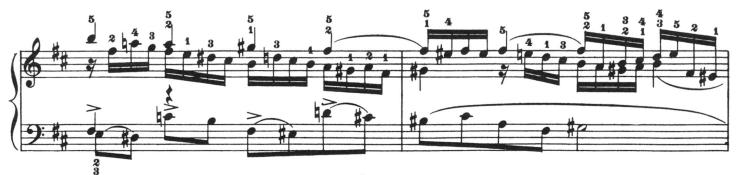

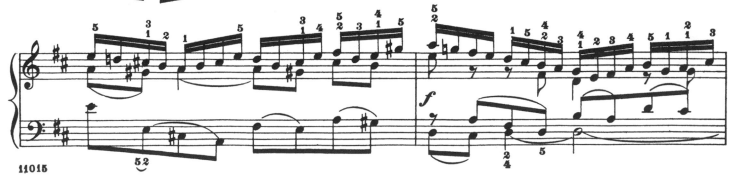

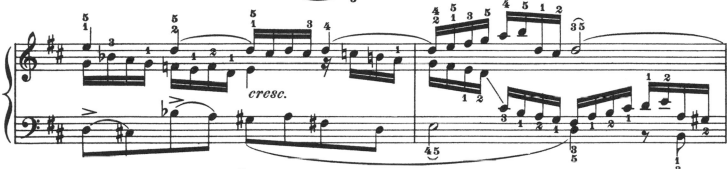

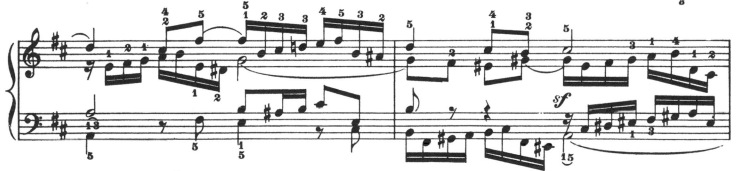

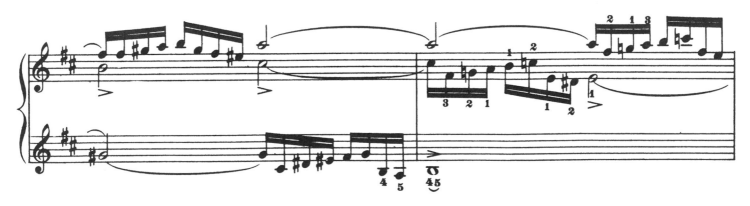